Collins

SCRABBLE

junior

BRAND CROSSWORD GAME

Advanced
Puzzles

Get ready for more than
120 word puzzles!

With 2 levels of play just like
the **SCRABBLE**™ Junior board game,
you can have a go at beginner level
puzzles or more challenging
advanced ones.

On this side, you'll find the
advanced puzzles. Looking
for the beginner ones?
Just turn the book over!

You'll find all the answers
in the middle of the book.

WORD DETECTIVE

Link the tiles to make as many words with three letters or more as you can. The letters can be linked in any direction - across, up, down or diagonally but you can't use the same tile twice in one word. Can you find the nine-letter word?

t	v	k	i
e	a	t	p
i	r	i	w
m	m	e	d

....

....

....

....

....

....

WORD BUILDER

How many words of three-letters or more can you make out of the tiles below?

d e o h s m y

....

....

....

....

....

....

....

....

....

....

ARROW WORDS

Work out the answers to the clues and write them in the grid, following the arrows.

Cooking pot	Large primate	▼	Break	▼	Undo a knot
▶	▼		Money set aside for later use		What a painter creates
E.g. spaghetti ▶			▼		▼
▶					
Fix or mend	Part of the eye	Animal doctor ▶			
▶	▼			A snake-like fish	Attempt
Small; tiny	Item for catching fish ▶			▼	▼
▶					
Spice with a hot taste		Crafty and cunning ▶			

SNAKEWORD

Draw a continous line through the tiles below to spell out the hidden nine-letter word. Any of the tiles could be the first letter, and the line can only pass through each tile once.

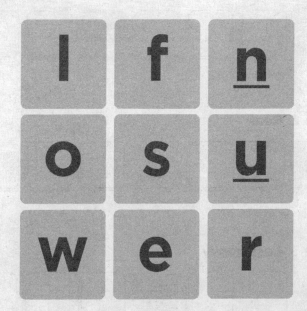

l	f	n̲
o	s	u̲
w	e	r

Write the word here.

GIVE ME A CLUE

Can you fill in the blank tiles
to create a word that solves
each of the clues below?

Clue 1 Salad vegetable

Clue 2 Real

Clue 3 Less heavy

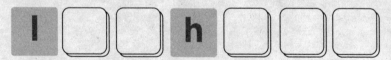

Clue 4 Most simple

KRISS KROSS

Place all of the words in the list below into the empty tiles. Use each word once to complete the puzzle.

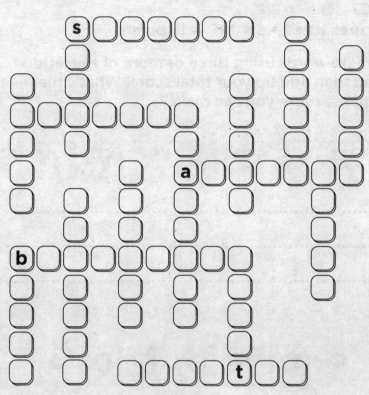

5 LETTERS
bored
brave
eager
light
scary
upset
wrong

6 LETTERS
better
hungry

7 LETTERS
annoyed
excited
fragile

7 LETTERS cont'd
perfect
strange

8 LETTERS
thankful

9 LETTERS
beautiful

SCRABBLE™ SCORE

In Scrabble you score points for the letters you use in making words, for example:

Z₁₀ E₁ B₃ R₁ A₁

Scores 10 + 1 + 3 + 1 + 1 = 16 points

Create words using three or more of the letters and then add up your total score. What's the highest score you can make?

R₁ B₃ E₁ A₁ N₁ V₄ T₁

....

....

....

R₁ O₁ F₄ B₃ F₄ D₂ A₁

....

....

....

WORD SPLITS

These three words have been split into three parts and reordered. Can you put the parts in the right order to make the original word?

re | me | a | s | u

iu | m | t | r | p | h

a | r | d | s | t | c | u

MISSING VOWELS

All vowels have been removed from each word below and are shown at the side. Can you put them back in to recreate the words?

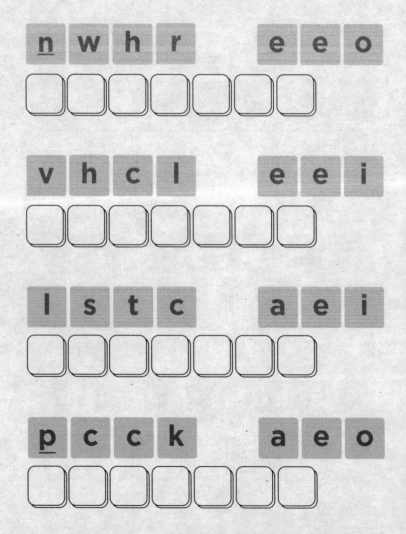

n w h r   e e o

v h c l   e e i

l s t c   a e i

p c c k   a e o

STAR LETTERS

Work out the seven-letter word, using each Scrabble tile once and the star tile twice. There are three words for you to find. The first letter has been filled in for you.

a m d c o n

c _ _ _ _ _ _

e r l i t g

g _ _ _ _ _ _

r b i h s u

r _ _ _ _ _ _

WORD SCRAMBLE

Rearrange the Scrabble tiles to create four words.
(Hint: these are all farming words.)

l e <u>d</u> i f

<u>p</u> h e s e

m a f r e r

a t c r o t r

GIVE ME A CLUE

Can you fill in the blank tiles to create a word that solves each of the clues below?

Clue 1 Difficulty

| t | | | | b | | |

Clue 2 Nose part

| n | | | | | | l |

Clue 3 Very old

| a | | | i | | | |

Clue 4 Vegetable

| c | | b | | | | |

WORDSEARCH

Find all the words from the list below in the grid. Words may appear horizontally, vertically or diagonally and in either a forwards or backwards direction.

t	n	h	o	p	c	g	e	z	t	o	z
a	p	o	n	u	e	p	o	s	k	e	m
c	w	r	i	g	o	u	v	a	b	z	h
u	o	s	n	l	t	s	u	r	t	a	y
t	a	e	e	o	o	r	a	g	n	a	k
a	w	t	v	r	z	h	l	a	p	l	q
a	n	x	r	a	j	r	z	g	e	m	t
a	w	u	d	k	i	d	i	w	e	o	b
i	t	n	a	h	p	e	l	e	h	n	e
c	a	x	l	o	s	c	o	w	s	k	r
p	r	l	i	s	q	p	s	d	j	e	i
h	i	e	s	o	o	g	n	o	m	y	t

antelope	**lion**
cow	**mongoose**
elephant	**monkey**
goat	**panda**
horse	**sheep**
kangaroo	**zebra**

SCRABBLE™ SCORE

In Scrabble you score points for the letters you use in making words, for example:

Z_{10} E_1 B_3 R_1 A_1

Scores 10 + 1 + 3 + 1 + 1 = 16 points

Create words using three or more of the letters and then add up your total score. What's the highest score you can make?

B_3 I_1 U_1 K_5 C_3 Q_{10} E_1

....

....

....

E_1 N_1 Y_4 M_3 K_5 O_1 G_2

....

....

....

ARROW WORDS

Work out the answers to the clues and write them in the grid, following the arrows.

The one after this one	Reflection of a sound	Image that shows your bones (1-3)	Container	Money owed	▼
▶	▼	▼	▼	Event that did not seem possible	
Tiny piece of bread ▶				▼	
Routine act; custom ▶					
▶			Enclose a gift in paper		Shout or scream loudly
Male child	Item used to play snooker	Method of doing something	▼		▼
▶	▼				
Rare		Every ▶			
Remove from school ▶					

WORD DETECTIVE

Link the tiles to make as many words with three letters or more as you can. The letters can be linked in any direction - across, up, down or diagonally but you can't use the same tile twice in one word. Can you find the nine-letter word?

s	j	l	a
x	a	r	c
t	i	h	t
z	e	c	r

....

....

....

....

....

....

KRISS KROSS

Place all of the words in the list below into the empty tiles. Use each word once to complete the puzzle.

3 LETTERS
eel

4 LETTERS
clam
crab
kelp

5 LETTERS
shark
squid
whale

6 LETTERS
mussel
shells

7 LETTERS
haddock
herring
lobster
octopus

8 LETTERS
seahorse
starfish

9 LETTERS
jellyfish

WORD BUILDER

How many words of three-letters or more can you make out of the tiles below?

t p i e r a d

....
....
....
....
....
....
....
....
....
....

SCRABBLE™ SCORE

In Scrabble you score points for the letters you use in making words, for example:

Z_{10} E_1 B_3 R_1 A_1

Scores 10 + 1 + 3 + 1 + 1 = 16 points

Create words using three or more of the letters and then add up your total score. What's the highest score you can make?

E_1 C_3 R_1 O_1 I_1 M_3 C_3

....
....
....

I_1 D_2 N_1 P_3 B_3 E_1 H_4

....
....
....

WORD SCRAMBLE

Rearrange the Scrabble tiles to create four words.
(Hint: these are all birds.)

a e l e g

o i r b n

t p a r o r

s o t c i r h

STAR LETTERS

Work out the seven-letter word, using each Scrabble tile once and the star tile twice. There are three words for you to find. The first letter has been filled in for you.

SNAKEWORD

Draw a continous line through the tiles below to spell out the hidden nine-letter word. Any of the tiles could be the first letter, and the line can only pass through each tile once.

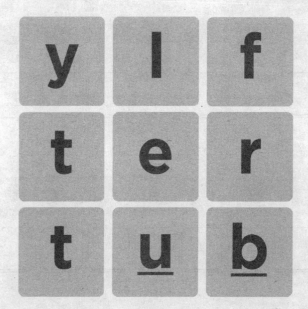

y	l	f
t	e	r
t	<u>u</u>	<u>b</u>

Write the word here.

WORD SPLITS

These three words have been split into three parts and reordered. Can you put the parts in the right order to make the original word?

s i   o u t   d e

s u   s s   c c e

r y   t e   m y s

WORDSEARCH

Find all the words from the list below in the grid. Words may appear horizontally, vertically or diagonally and in either a forwards or backwards direction.

t	w	b	t	e	b	x	c	u	y	i	h
t	r	e	c	o	s	t	u	m	e	c	s
n	r	e	r	i	s	n	r	k	t	w	e
p	o	e	z	e	g	t	i	i	e	i	y
y	u	r	b	f	w	s	w	e	o	t	w
q	m	m	d	a	j	o	t	w	w	s	p
p	a	m	p	l	t	s	l	m	n	o	s
z	t	o	u	k	u	o	y	f	s	h	w
h	n	d	v	m	i	a	x	t	w	g	f
l	o	a	r	s	l	n	c	o	r	r	p
r	o	c	k	e	i	b	m	o	z	a	h
q	m	a	n	f	o	d	e	v	t	t	p

bat

party

cauldron

pumpkin

costume

sweets

ghost

werewolf

moon

witch

mummy

zombie

WORD BUILDER

How many words of three-letters or more can you make out of the tiles below?

s t n h u d e

....

....

....

....

....

....

....

....

....

....

SCRABBLE™ SCORE

In Scrabble you score points for the letters you use in making words, for example:

Z₁₀ E₁ B₃ R₁ A₁

Scores 10 + 1 + 3 + 1 + 1 = 16 points

Create words using three or more of the letters and then add up your total score. What's the highest score you can make?

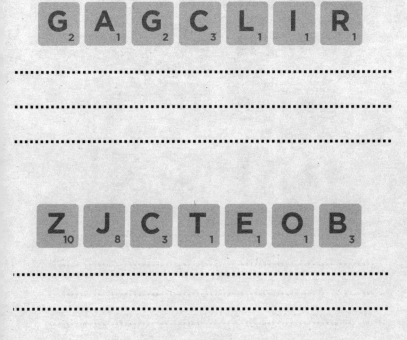

G₂ A₁ G₂ C₃ L₁ I₁ R₁

....

....

....

Z₁₀ J₈ C₃ T₁ E₁ O₁ B₃

....

....

....

WORD DETECTIVE

Link the tiles to make as many words with three letters or more as you can. The letters can be linked in any direction - across, up, down or diagonally but you can't use the same tile twice in one word. Can you find the nine-letter word?

m	t	g	<u>n</u>
u	h	i	o
r	r	l	l
z	i	l	e

....

....

....

....

....

....

MISSING VOWELS

All vowels have been removed from each word below and are shown at the side. Can you put them back in to recreate the words?

r n b w   a i o

p c t r   e i u

y n g r   e o u

j r n y   e o u

ARROW WORDS

Work out the answers to the clues and write them in the grid, following the arrows.

Great happiness	Item used to row a boat	▼	Write using a keyboard	▼	Award
►	▼		Frequent		Allow to happen
Fourth month ►			▼		▼
►					
Gentle wind	School test	Acquire; obtain ►			
►	▼			Half of two	Opposite of good
List of food options		Tennis shot ►		▼	▼
►					
Yellow fruit		Primary colour ►			

KRISS KROSS

Place all of the words in the list below into the empty tiles. Use each word once to complete the puzzle.

3 LETTERS
jay

4 LETTERS
coot
crow
ibis
swan
wren

5 LETTERS
goose
grebe
raven
robin

7 LETTERS
chicken
pelican
penguin
sparrow
swallow

9 LETTERS
albatross
chaffinch
cormorant

SCRABBLE™ SCORE

In Scrabble you score points for the letters you use in making words, for example:

Z₁₀ E₁ B₃ R₁ A₁

Scores 10 + 1 + 3 + 1 + 1 = 16 points

Create words using three or more of the letters and then add up your total score. What's the highest score you can make?

C₃ C₃ N₁ A₁ U₁ R₁ H₄

....

....

....

T₁ E₁ J₈ K₅ C₃ T₁ A₁

....

....

....

STAR LETTERS

Work out the seven-letter word, using each Scrabble tile once and the star tile twice. There are three words for you to find. The first letter has been filled in for you.

SNAKEWORD

Draw a continous line through the tiles below to spell out the hidden nine-letter word. Any of the tiles could be the first letter, and the line can only pass through each tile once.

s	h	a
k	m	k
l	i	e

Write the word here.

GIVE ME A CLUE

Can you fill in the blank tiles to create a word that solves each of the clues below?

Clue 1 Not deep

Clue 2 Flowers on a tree

Clue 3 Rich

Clue 4 Flightless bird

STAR LETTERS

Work out the seven-letter word, using each Scrabble tile once and the star tile twice. There are three words for you to find. The first letter has been filled in for you.

WORD BUILDER

How many words of three-letters or more can you make out of the tiles below?

m p o r l a s

....

....

....

....

....

....

....

....

....

....

WORD SCRAMBLE

Rearrange the Scrabble tiles to create four words.
(Hint: these are all words to do with jewellery.)

WORD SPLITS

These three words have been split into three parts and reordered. Can you put the parts in the right order to make the original word?

g e | <u>p</u> a | c k a

<u>n</u> c | i | <u>n</u> g | <u>d</u> a

a w | e | s e | e <u>d</u>

WORDSEARCH

Find all the words from the list below in the grid. Words may appear horizontally, vertically or diagonally and in either a forwards or backwards direction.

e	o	r	a	v	t	u	r	k	e	y	i
c	b	r	o	c	c	o	l	i	r	c	o
h	a	c	t	e	w	l	c	s	s	t	y
i	o	e	a	o	a	u	q	u	t	a	v
c	t	g	c	m	r	k	a	z	d	a	a
k	a	a	b	p	a	r	s	n	i	p	r
e	t	b	m	e	j	t	a	r	a	p	g
n	o	b	z	v	r	e	i	c	r	o	l
p	p	a	c	s	t	u	f	f	i	n	g
t	e	c	y	y	l	t	r	w	p	u	a
z	o	a	o	q	r	e	o	p	c	r	t
l	z	b	s	k	b	e	e	f	p	o	q

beef	**lamb**
broccoli	**parsnip**
cabbage	**pea**
carrot	**potato**
chicken	**stuffing**
gravy	**turkey**

WORD DETECTIVE

Link the tiles to make as many words with three letters or more as you can. The letters can be linked in any direction - across, up, down or diagonally but you can't use the same tile twice in one word. Can you find the nine-letter word?

u	i	t	a
q	w	r	n
n	a	i	o
i	m	a	t

....

....

....

....

....

....

WORDSEARCH

Find all the words from the list below in the grid. Words may appear horizontally, vertically or diagonally and in either a forwards or backwards direction.

```
c n p a r r o t v i g i
r i t t y c s a z e s r
a p u t f e e a r s d a
u a c a t s b l l l l
b r l m e o i r c z j u
r r m g o l d f i s h t
a e p l a j k e m a a n
b t t n i t c r l h s a
b x k s y z s i l p n r
i u t m m b a g o d a a
t t p p e a p r t s k t
j m o u s e h r d i e b
```

cat
dog
gerbil
goldfish
hamster
lizard

mouse
parrot
rabbit
snake
tarantula
terrapin

ARROW WORDS

Work out the answers to the clues and write them in the grid, following the arrows.

Small dot	Poem writer ▼	Solely; merely ▼	Draw ▼	Desire to have	▼
▶				Shape with eight sides	
Type of vegetable ▶				▼	
Choose a politician for office ▶					
▶			First light in the morning		Refuse to admit
Home for a pig	Type of hat	Father ▶	▼		▼
▶	▼				
Historical cold period (3,3)		Came first ▶			
Low- value coin ▶					

GIVE ME A CLUE

Can you fill in the blank tiles to create a word that solves each of the clues below?

Clue 1 Green gem

Clue 2 Great joy

Clue 3 Musical instrument

Clue 4 Always

KRISS KROSS

Place all of the words in the list below into the empty tiles. Use each word once to complete the puzzle.

4 LETTERS
iris
lily
rose
stem

5 LETTERS
daisy
lilac
pansy
peony
petal
poppy
stalk

6 LETTERS
clover
leaves
orchid

7 LETTERS
begonia
petunia

8 LETTERS
primrose

9 LETTERS
buttercup

WORD BUILDER

How many words of three-letters or more can you make out of the tiles below?

Tiles: s t a e w r c

....

....

....

....

....

....

....

....

....

....

WORD SPLITS

These three words have been split into three parts and reordered. Can you put the parts in the right order to make the original word?

d o | **i n** | **l p h**

d i | **r e a** | **n g**

n i m m | **m i** | **u m**

MISSING VOWELS

All vowels have been removed from each word below and are shown at the side. Can you put them back in to recreate the words?

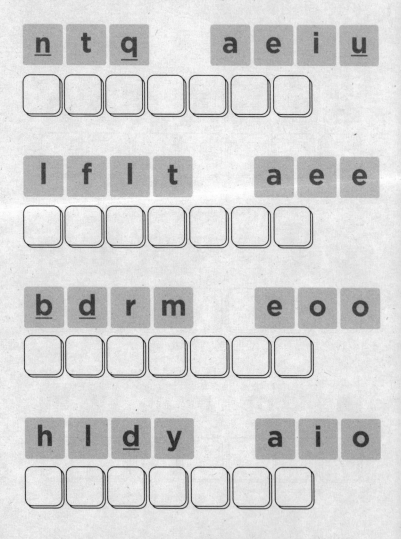

STAR LETTERS

Work out the seven-letter word, using each Scrabble tile once and the star tile twice. There are three words for you to find. The first letter has been filled in for you.

☆r u e a l q

q _ _ _ _ _ _

k g c i **☆o** n

c _ _ _ _ _ _

r **☆t** e n w i

w _ _ _ _ _ _

WORD DETECTIVE

Link the tiles to make as many words with three letters or more as you can. The letters can be linked in any direction - across, up, down or diagonally but you can't use the same tile twice in one word. Can you find the nine-letter word?

....

....

....

....

....

....

GIVE ME A CLUE

Can you fill in the blank tiles to create a word that solves each of the clues below?

Clue 1 Bravery

Clue 2 100 years

Clue 3 E.g. London or Paris

Clue 4 Get rid of

WORDSEARCH

Find all the words from the list below in the grid. Words may appear horizontally, vertically or diagonally and in either a forwards or backwards direction.

x	a	l	p	s	u	n	s	h	i	n	e
s	e	i	l	f	r	e	t	t	u	b	p
p	p	u	l	i	p	n	j	g	i	m	b
s	x	s	w	s	h	d	n	u	p	u	a
w	h	g	l	c	w	i	e	s	i	x	r
i	a	o	a	e	x	o	i	r	c	h	b
m	f	e	l	a	v	e	o	o	n	t	e
m	b	o	l	i	a	a	n	o	i	m	c
i	a	e	v	t	d	f	r	d	c	r	u
n	r	a	l	l	t	a	j	t	t	a	e
g	s	t	u	b	f	a	y	u	p	w	b
z	d	t	s	e	a	s	h	o	r	e	r

barbeque
beach
butterflies
holiday
outdoors
picnic

relaxing
seashore
sunshine
swimming
travel
warmth

SCRABBLE™ SCORE

In Scrabble you score points for the letters you use in making words, for example:

Scores 10 + 1 + 3 + 1 + 1 = 16 points

Create words using three or more of the letters and then add up your total score. What's the highest score you can make?

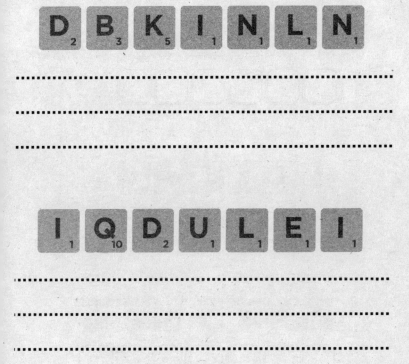

WORD SCRAMBLE

Rearrange the Scrabble tiles to create four words.
(Hint: these are all jobs.)

a e r k b

o r d t c o

r i a t s t

r e d u l b i

SNAKEWORD

Draw a continous line through the tiles below to spell out the hidden nine-letter word. Any of the tiles could be the first letter, and the line can only pass through each tile once.

e	a	t
l	<u>b</u>	e
v	e	g

Write the word here.

ARROW WORDS

Work out the answers to the clues and write them in the grid, following the arrows.

Completely level	Get beaten	Performs on stage	Hot drink	Solid ground	▼
▶	▼	▼	▼	Worried; uneasy	
A large sea ▶				▼	
Opposite of sit ▶					
▶			Green citrus fruit		Finishes
Opposite of no	Help or support	A false statement ▶	▼		▼
▶	▼				
Country		Dirt ▶			
Put clothes on ▶					

KRISS KROSS

Place all of the words in the list below into the empty tiles. Use each word once to complete the puzzle.

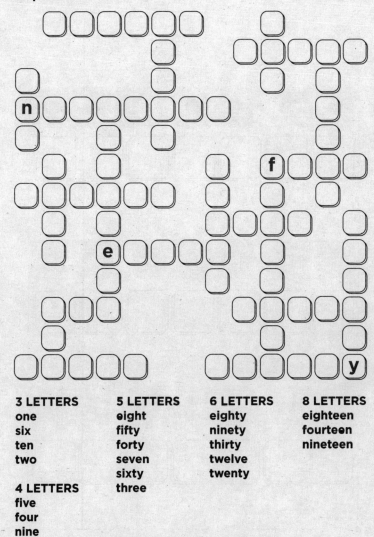

3 LETTERS
one
six
ten
two

4 LETTERS
five
four
nine

5 LETTERS
eight
fifty
forty
seven
sixty
three

6 LETTERS
eighty
ninety
thirty
twelve
twenty

8 LETTERS
eighteen
fourteen
nineteen

WORD SPLITS

These three words have been split into three parts and reordered. Can you put the parts in the right order to make the original word?

WORD SCRAMBLE

Rearrange the Scrabble tiles to create four words.
(Hint: these are all mythical words.)

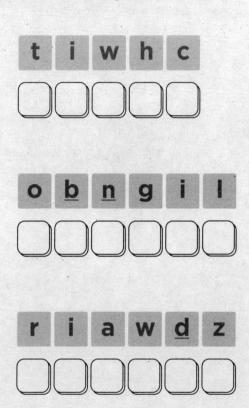

ADVANCED PUZZLE ANSWERS

Page 4 – Word Detective

**nine-letter word
immediate**

*there are lots of other
possible words e.g.*
**edit, media, aimed,
pirate and trimmed**

Page 6 – Arrow Words

		s		u	
p	a	n		n	
	p	a	s	t	a
r	e	p	a	i	r
			v	e	t
m	i	n	i		
	r		n	e	t
g	i	n	g	e	r
	s		s	l	y

Page 5 – Word Builder

*There are lots of
possible words, here
are a few:*
**hoe, demo, mode,
home and shoe**

Page 7 – Snakeword

sunflower

Page 8 – Give Me a Clue

1 lettuce
2 genuine
3 lighter
4 easiest

Page 10 – SCRABBLE™ Score

There are lots of possible words but the highest scoring words are:

BRAVE 10 pts
AFFORD 13 pts

Page 9 – Kriss Kross

Page 11 – Word Splits

measure
triumph
custard

Page 12 – Missing Vowels

nowhere
vehicle
elastic
peacock

Page 14 – Word Scramble

field
sheep
farmer
tractor

Page 13 – Star Letters

command
glitter
rubbish

Page 15 – Give Me a Clue

1 trouble
2 nostril
3 ancient
4 cabbage

Page 16 – Wordsearch

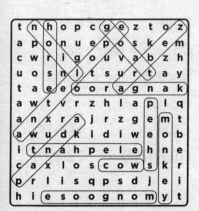

Page 18 – Arrow Words

						d
n	e	x	t			e
	c	r	u	m	b	b
	h	a	b	i	t	t
b	o	y		r		
		w	a	y		
s	c	a	r	c	e	
	u		a	l	l	
	e	x	p	e	l	

Page 17 – SCRABBLE™ Score

There are lots of possible words but the highest scoring words are:

QUICK	20 pts
MONKEY	15 pts

Page 19 – Word Detective

nine-letter word
architect

there are lots of other possible words e.g. ache, chair, crate, irate and tiara

Page 20 – Kriss Kross

```
w       c     m u s s e l
h       r           h
a       a           a     j
l o b s t e r       r     e
e               k e l p         s
                    l           e
h a d d o c k       y           a
e           c       f           h
r       s t a r f i s h         o
r       o           s           r
i       p           s h e l l s
n   s q u i d           e       e
g       s               c l a m
```

Page 22 – SCRABBLE™ Score

There are lots of possible words but the highest scoring words are:

COMIC 11 pts

BEHIND 12 pts

Page 21 – Word Builder

There are lots of possible words, here are a few:

air, pie, pier, raid and tier

Page 23 – Word Scramble

eagle

robin

parrot

ostrich

Page 24 – Star Letters

channel
witness
shuffle

Page 26 – Word Splits

outside
success
mystery

Page 25 – Snakeword

butterfly

Page 27 – Wordsearch

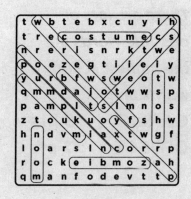

Page 28 – Word Builder

There are lots of possible words, here are a few:
hut, dent, hunt, sent and shut

Page 30 – Word Detective

nine-letter word
thrilling

there are lots of other possible words e.g.
girl, hill, night, thing and hurling

Page 29 – SCRABBLE™ Score

There are lots of possible words but the highest scoring words are:

GARLIC   9 pts
OBJECT   17 pts

Page 31 – Missing Vowels

rainbow
picture
younger
journey

Page 32 – Arrow Words

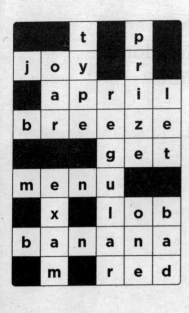

Page 34 – SCRABBLE™ Score

There are lots of possible words but the highest scoring words are:

CRUNCH   13 pts

JACKET   19 pts

Page 33 – Kriss Kross

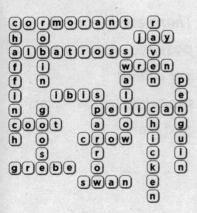

Page 35 – Star Letters

happily

comment

village

Page 36 – Snakeword

milkshake

Page 38 – Star Letters

allowed
freedom
fitness

Page 37 – Give Me a Clue

1 shallow
2 blossom
3 wealthy
4 penguin

Page 39 – Word Builder

There are lots of possible words, here are a few:
mop, sap, arms, lamp and slam

Page 40 – Word Scramble

beads
locket
bangle
earring

Page 41 – Word Splits

package
dancing
seaweed

Page 42 – Wordsearch

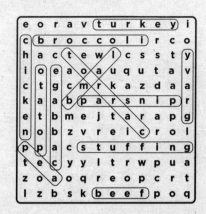

Page 43 – Word Detective

nine-letter word
animation

there are lots of other possible words e.g. main, roam, wait, warn and minor

Page 44 – Wordsearch

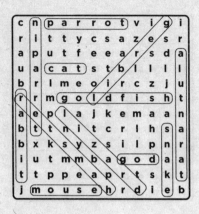

Page 46 – Give Me a Clue

1 emerald
2 delight
3 trumpet
4 forever

Page 45 – Arrow Words

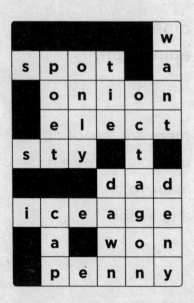

Page 47 – Kriss Kross

Page 48 – Word Builder

There are lots of possible words, here are a few:

eat, tea, cart, seat and water

Page 50 – Missing Vowels

antique
leaflet
bedroom
holiday

Page 49 – Word Splits

dolphin
reading
minimum

Page 51 – Star Letters

quarrel
cooking
written

Page 52 – Word Detective

nine-letter word
chocolate

there are lots of other
possible words e.g.
pat, claw, coat,
cool and late

Page 54 – Wordsearch

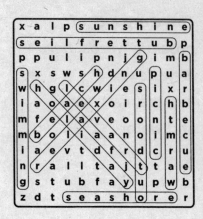

Page 53 – Give Me a Clue

1 courage
2 century
3 capital
4 abolish

Page 55 – SCRABBLE™ Score

There are lots of
possible words but
the highest scoring
words are:

BLINK   11 pts
LIQUID   16 pts

Page 56 – Word Scramble

baker
doctor
artist
builder

Page 58 – Arrow Words

					l
f	l	a	t		a
	o	c	e	a	n
	s	t	a	n	d
y	e	s		x	
			l	i	e
n	a	t	i	o	n
	i		m	u	d
	d	r	e	s	s

Page 57 – Snakeword

vegetable

Page 59 – Kriss Kross

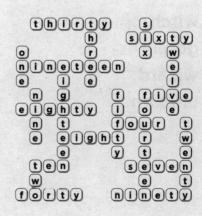

Page 60 – Word Splits

notepad
meeting
lobster

Page 61 – Word Scramble

witch
goblin
wizard
unicorn

NOTES

Collins

SCRABBLE™ junior
BRAND CROSSWORD GAME

Beginner Puzzles

Published by Collins
An imprint of HarperCollinsPublishers
Westerhill Road
Bishopbriggs
Glasgow G64 2QT
www.harpercollins.co.uk

HarperCollinsPublishers
1st Floor, Watermarque Building, Ringsend Road, Dublin 4, Ireland

All puzzles supplied by Clarity Media Ltd
All images © Shutterstock.com

First published in 2022

ISBN 978-0-00-852619-1

10 9 8 7 6 5 4 3 2 1

A catalogue record for this book is available from the British Library

Printed and bound in the UK using 100% renewable electricity at CPI Group (UK) Ltd

MIX
Paper | Supporting
responsible forestry
FSC™ C007454

This book is produced from independently certified FSC™ paper to ensure responsible forest management.

For more information visit: www.harpercollins.co.uk/green

Get ready for more than
120 word puzzles!

With 2 levels of play just like the
SCRABBLE™ Junior board game, you
can have a go at beginner level puzzles
or more challenging advanced ones.

On this side, you'll find the beginner
puzzles. Looking for the advanced ones?
Just turn the book over!

You'll find all the answers
in the middle of the book.

WORD DETECTIVE

Link the tiles to make as many words with three letters or more as you can. The letters can be linked in any direction - across, up, down or diagonally but you can't use the same tile twice in one word. Can you find the six-letter word?

f	e	c	i
y	t	r	v
g	j	l	d
s	e	a	r

....

....

....

....

....

....

ARROW WORDS

Work out the answers to the clues and write them in the grid, following the arrows.

Tap something lightly	Tree; fire residue	▼	Mix using a spoon	▼ h	Doglike wild animal
▶	▼	t	Aquatic mammal	y	Use a needle and thread
Teams	▶ s	i	d		▼
▶	h		o	n	
Royal chair	Attic	Legal rule	▶		
▶ f	▼	i	p	Frozen form of water	Animal foot
Turn over	o	Part of the body	▶	▼	▼
▶			i		
A continent		Opposite of old	▶ n		

GIVE ME A CLUE

Can you fill in the blank Scrabble tiles to complete the words? Use the clues to help.

Clue 1 Begin

	t		r	

Clue 2 Large bird of prey

e		g		

Clue 3 Popular board game

c	h			

Clue 4 Go inside

e		t		

KRISS KROSS

Place all of the words in the list below into the empty tiles. Use each word once to complete the puzzle.

5 LETTERS
rugby

6 LETTERS
diving
hockey
karate
squash

7 LETTERS
cricket
cycling
netball

10 LETTERS
basketball

MISSING VOWELS

All vowels have been removed from each word below and are shown at the side. Can you put them back in to recreate the words?

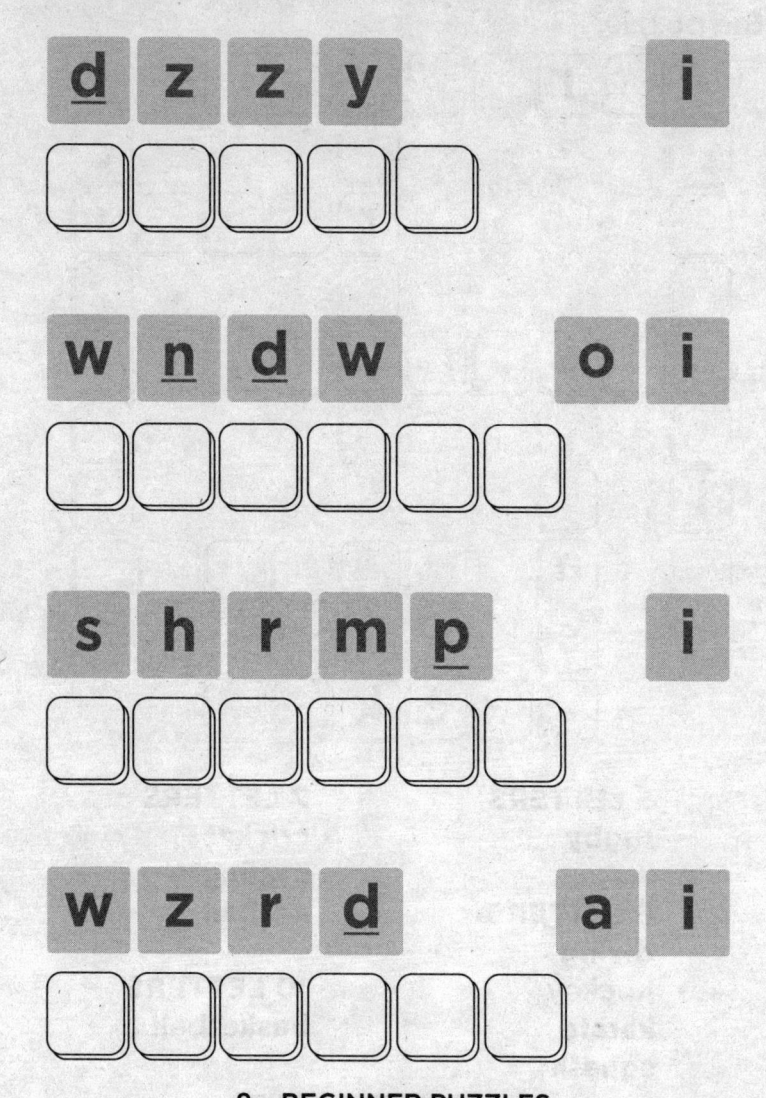

| d | z | z | y | | i |

| w | n | d | w | | o | i |

| s | h | r | m | p | | i |

| w | z | r | d | | a | i |

SNAKEWORD

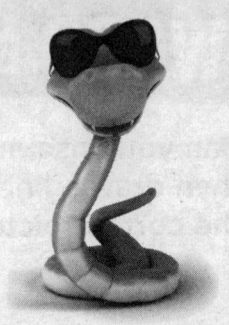

Draw a continous line through the tiles below to spell out the hidden six-letter word. Any of the tiles could be the first letter, and the line can only pass through each tile once.

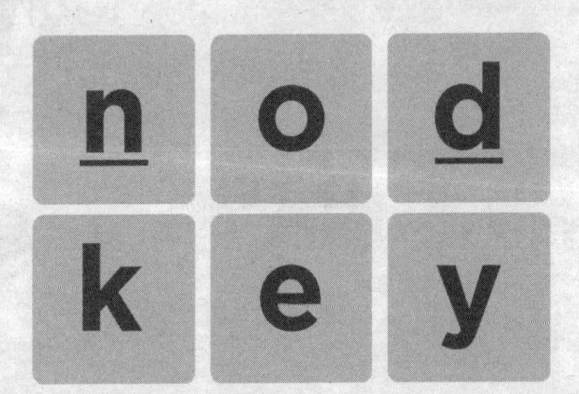

Write the word here.

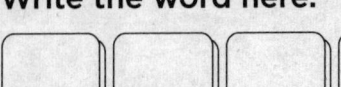

WORD MATCH

Can you unscramble each of the words and then draw a line to match each word with the correct picture?

o l s t h

e h e p s

i p d e s r

s n k e a

STAR LETTERS

Work out the five-letter word, using each Scrabble tile once and the star tile twice. There are three words for you to find. The first letter has been filled in for you.

WORD SCRAMBLE

Rearrange the Scrabble tiles to create four words.
(Hint: They are all animals.)

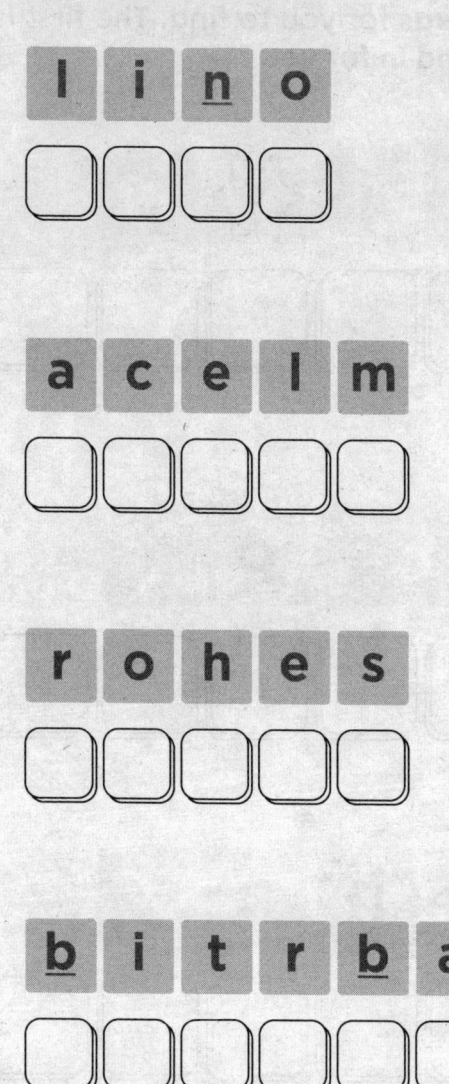

l i n o

a c e l m

r o h e s

b i t r b a

WORD SPLITS

These three words have been split into two or three parts and reordered. Can you put the parts in the right order to make the original word?

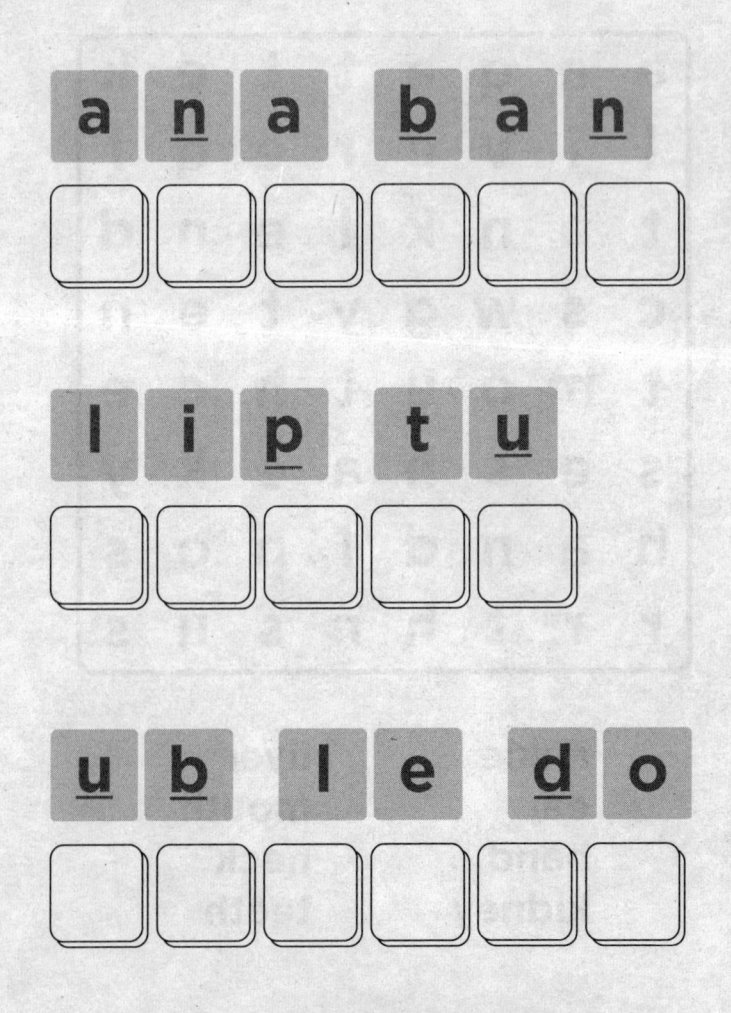

WORDSEARCH

Find all the words from the list below in the grid. Words may appear horizontally or vertically.

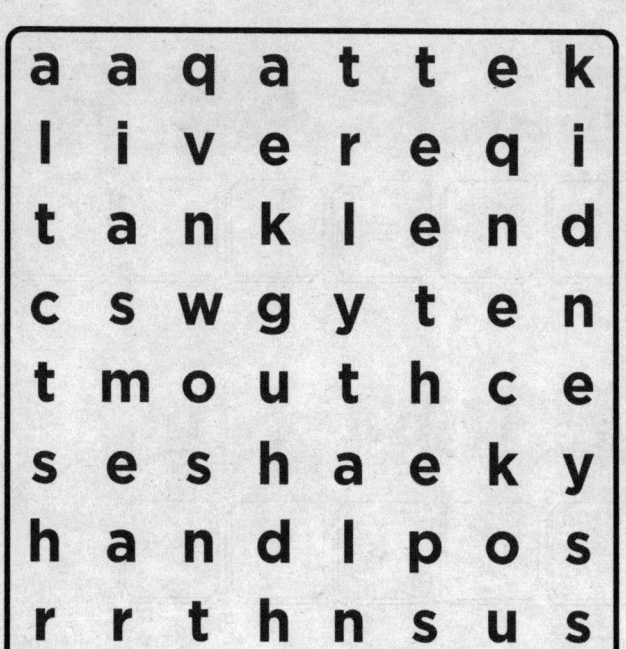

a	a	q	a	t	t	e	k
l	i	v	e	r	e	q	i
t	a	n	k	l	e	n	d
c	s	w	g	y	t	e	n
t	m	o	u	t	h	c	e
s	e	s	h	a	e	k	y
h	a	n	d	l	p	o	s
r	r	t	h	n	s	u	s

ankle	**liver**
ear	**mouth**
hand	**neck**
kidney	**teeth**

WORD LINK

Use all the letters in the circle to make a word that links onto the word already given.

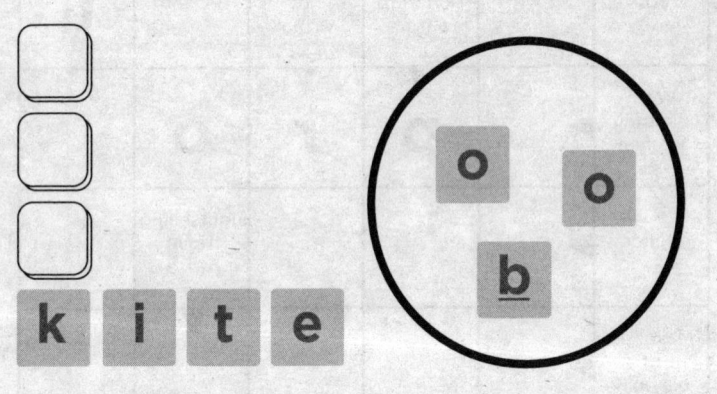

k i t e

Use all the letters in the circle to make a word that hooks the word already given – making two new words at once!

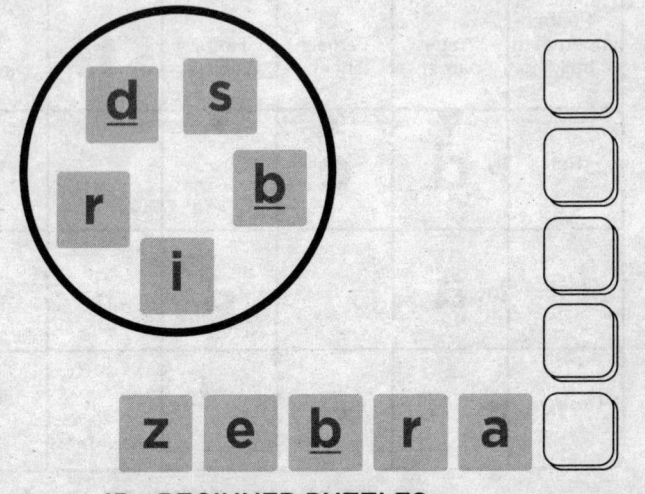

z e b r a

ARROW WORDS

Work out the answers to the clues and write them in the grid, following the arrows.

An item thrown away	▼	Remove skin from a fruit	Genuine; not virtual	Beneath	▼ u
Worn in the kitchen ▶		▼ p	▼ r	o	
Notice ▶			Sightseeing trip in Africa		
Make fun of playfully ▶			▼		
▶		l	a		r
Room underneath a building	Water barrier	Female sheep	Motor vehicle	f	Until now
Rot ▶ d	e	▼			▼ y
Alert ▶ a		a			
Deserve ▶	e				t

WORD DETECTIVE

Link the tiles to make as many words with three letters or more as you can. The letters can be linked in any direction - across, up, down or diagonally but you can't use the same tile twice in one word. Can you find the six-letter word?

o	w	l	<u>p</u>
<u>u</u>	h	t	l
j	a	<u>n</u>	z
l	<u>p</u>	<u>p</u>	e

....
....
....
....
....
....

KRISS KROSS

Place all of the words in the list below into the empty tiles. Use each word once to complete the puzzle.

3 LETTERS
art

4 LETTERS
bell
desk

5 LETTERS
books
chair
games
study

7 LETTERS
lessons
reading
subject

8 LETTERS
sandwich

WORD MATCH

Can you unscramble each of the words and then draw a line to match each word with the correct picture?

| l | l | _n_ | o | o | a | _b_ |

| e | k | c | a | s |

| i | g | t | f | s |

| a | e | l | _d_ | _n_ | c |

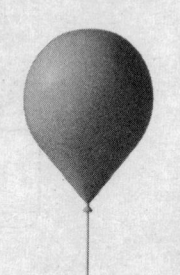

STAR LETTERS

Work out the five-letter word, using each Scrabble tile once and the star tile twice. There are three words for you to find. The first letter has been filled in for you.

h w e l

w _ _ _ _

u n y f

f _ _ _ _

i l g o

i _ _ _ _

GIVE ME A CLUE

Can you fill in the blank Scrabble tiles to complete the words? Use the clues to help.

Clue 1 Male relative

| | n | | l | |

Clue 2 Italian food

| p | | | z | |

Clue 3 Liquid

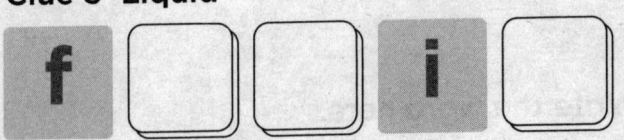

| f | | | i | |

Clue 4 Sandy area

| | e | a | | |

SNAKEWORD

Draw a continous line through the tiles below to spell out the hidden six-letter word. Any of the tiles could be the first letter, and the line can only pass through each tile once.

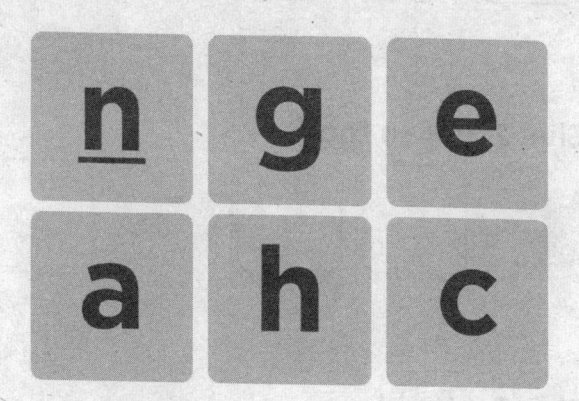

Write the word here.

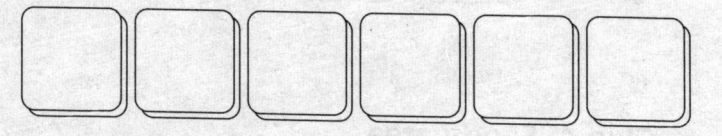

WORD SCRAMBLE

Rearrange the Scrabble tiles to create four words.
(Hint: They are all words about ocean animals.)

h i s f

□ □ □ □

a h e l w

□ □ □ □ □

r k h a s

□ □ □ □ □

s w u r l a

□ □ □ □ □ □

WORD SPLITS

These three words have been split into two or three parts and reordered. Can you put the parts in the right order to make the original word?

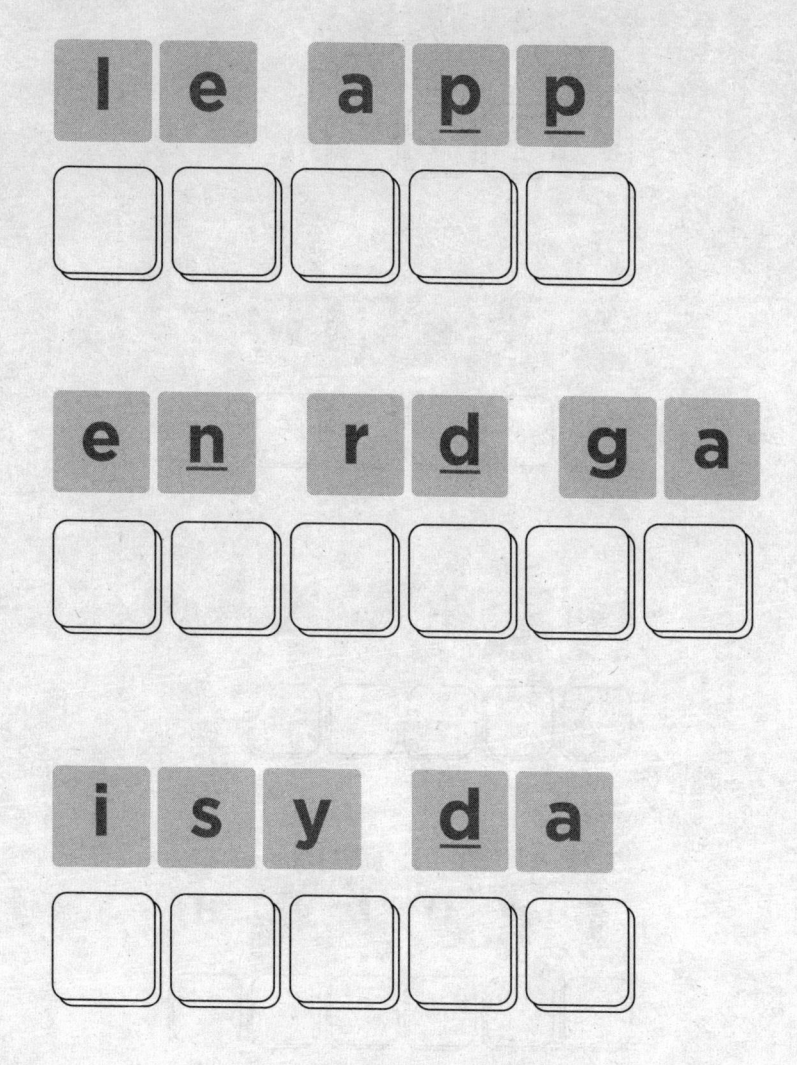

l e   a   p p

e   n   r   d   g   a

i   s   y   d   a

WORDSEARCH

Find all the words from the
list below in the grid. Words
may appear horizontally
or vertically.

b	t	m	e	o	a	u	k
a	w	i	e	m	l	l	j
c	j	l	a	e	t	t	b
o	o	k	h	l	o	a	a
n	c	e	r	e	a	l	n
d	s	l	v	t	s	w	a
e	g	g	s	t	t	a	n
p	j	a	m	e	s	j	a

bacon   jam
banana   milk
cereal   omelette
eggs   toast

WORD LINK

Use all the letters in the circle to make a word that links onto the word already given.

c a m p

Use all the letters in the circle to make a word that hooks the word already given – making two new words at once!

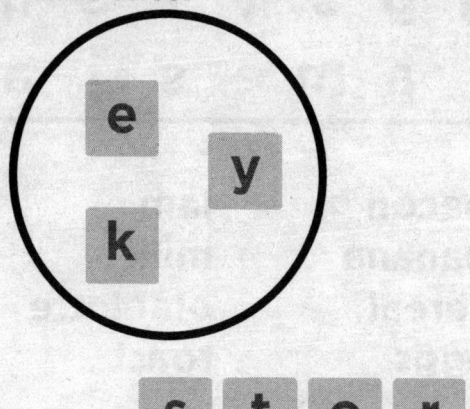

s t o r m

ARROW WORDS

Work out the answers to the clues and write them in the grid, following the arrows.

Large body of water	Hearing organ	▼ p	Light in colour	▼	Fun; enjoyment
► s	▼		Nocturnal flying animal		Adult males
Collection of songs	►	l	▼	u	▼ m
►		e		s	
Oily substance	Clean by rubbing with a cloth	Nine plus one	►		n
Move restlessly	▼ w	Not very bright	Space between two objects	m	An object you play with
►	i	▼	▼		▼
A large musical instrument	► p			n	
Containing nothing	►	m	p		

27 – BEGINNER PUZZLES

WORD DETECTIVE

Link the tiles to make as many words with three letters or more as you can. The letters can be linked in any direction - across, up, down or diagonally but you can't use the same tile twice in one word. Can you find the six-letter word?

c	o	y	x
p	l	j	m
t	e	k	n
i	v	e	r

....

....

....

....

....

....

KRISS KROSS

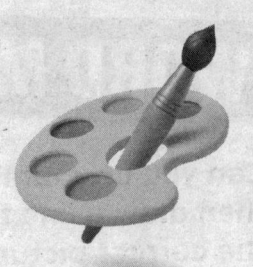

Place all of the words in the list below into the empty tiles. Use each word once to complete the puzzle.

4 LETTERS
blue
gold
grey

5 LETTERS
brown
green
lemon
white

6 LETTERS
purple
violet
yellow

9 LETTERS
turquoise

WORD MATCH

Can you unscramble each of the words and then draw a line to match each word with the correct picture?

l o <u>n</u> w c

a <u>b</u> c o a r t

<u>n</u> o <u>p</u> <u>p</u> r o c

r e l u j g g

STAR LETTERS

Work out the six-letter word, using each
Scrabble tile once and the star tile twice. There
are three words for you to find. The first letter
has been filled in for you.

WORDSEARCH

Find all the words from the list below in the grid. Words may appear horizontally or vertically.

s	p	e	l	l	s	k	f
v	v	c	a	r	d	s	o
r	a	w	s	t	a	g	e
e	n	i	w	a	n	d	o
x	i	z	p	r	o	p	s
v	s	a	l	z	s	t	j
c	h	r	s	c	s	z	d
j	s	d	o	v	e	s	w

cards   stage
doves   vanish
props   wand
spell   wizard

WORD SPLITS

These three words have been split into two or three parts and reordered. Can you put the parts in the right order to make the original word?

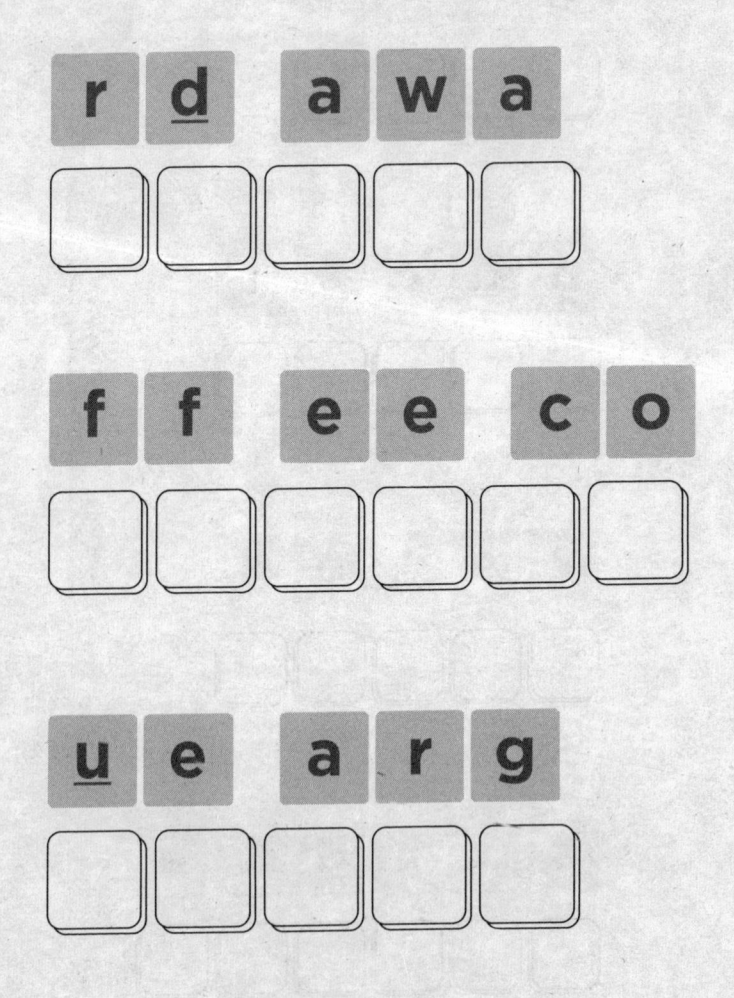

r d   a w a

f f   e e   c o

u e   a r g

WORD SCRAMBLE

Rearrange the Scrabble tiles to create four words.
(Hint: They are all words about Christmas.)

e t e r

□ □ □ □

a d c s r

□ □ □ □ □

v e l e s

□ □ □ □ □

s i h g l e

□ □ □ □ □ □

GIVE ME A CLUE

Can you fill in the blank Scrabble
tiles to complete the words?
Use the clues to help.

Clue 1 Citrus fruit

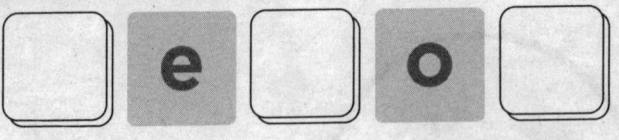

Clue 2 Opposite of below

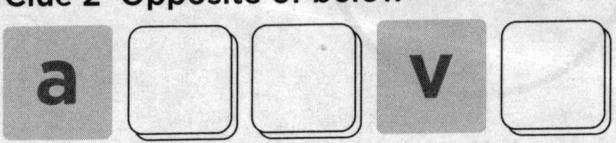

Clue 3 Keen

Clue 4 Young dog

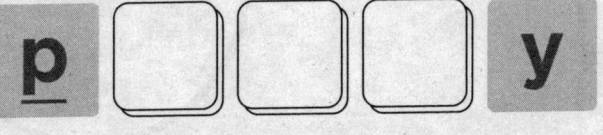

WORD LINK

Use all the letters in the circle
to make a word that links onto
the word already given.

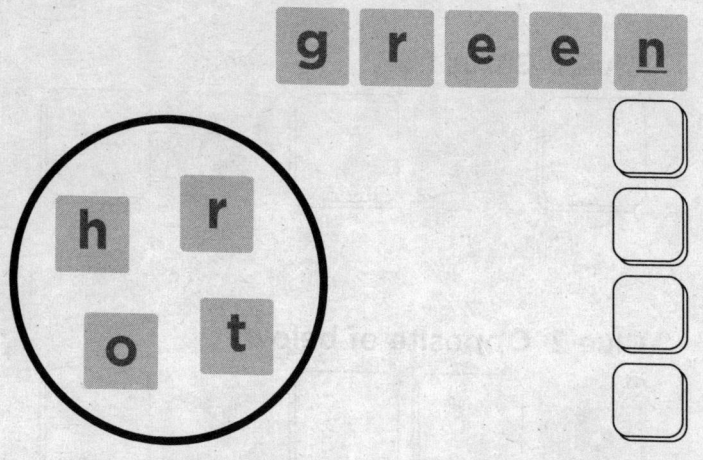

g r e e <u>n</u>

h r o t

Use all the letters in the circle to make a word
that hooks the word already given – making two
new words at once!

e a t

a s <u>p</u> t a

WORD MATCH

Can you unscramble each of the words and then draw a line to match each word with the correct picture?

v i l o n i

n i p o a

t l e u f

g t a u i r

MISSING VOWELS

All vowels have been removed from each word below and are shown at the side. Can you put them back in to recreate the words?

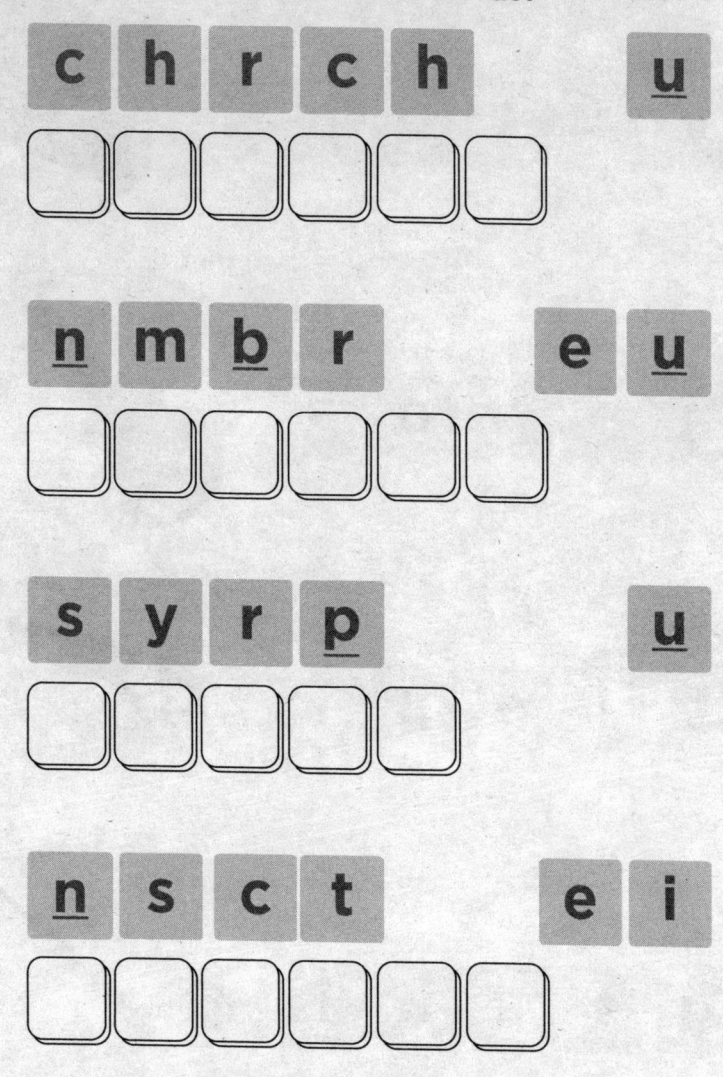

WORD SPLITS

These three words have been split into two or three parts and reordered. Can you put the parts in the right order to make the original word?

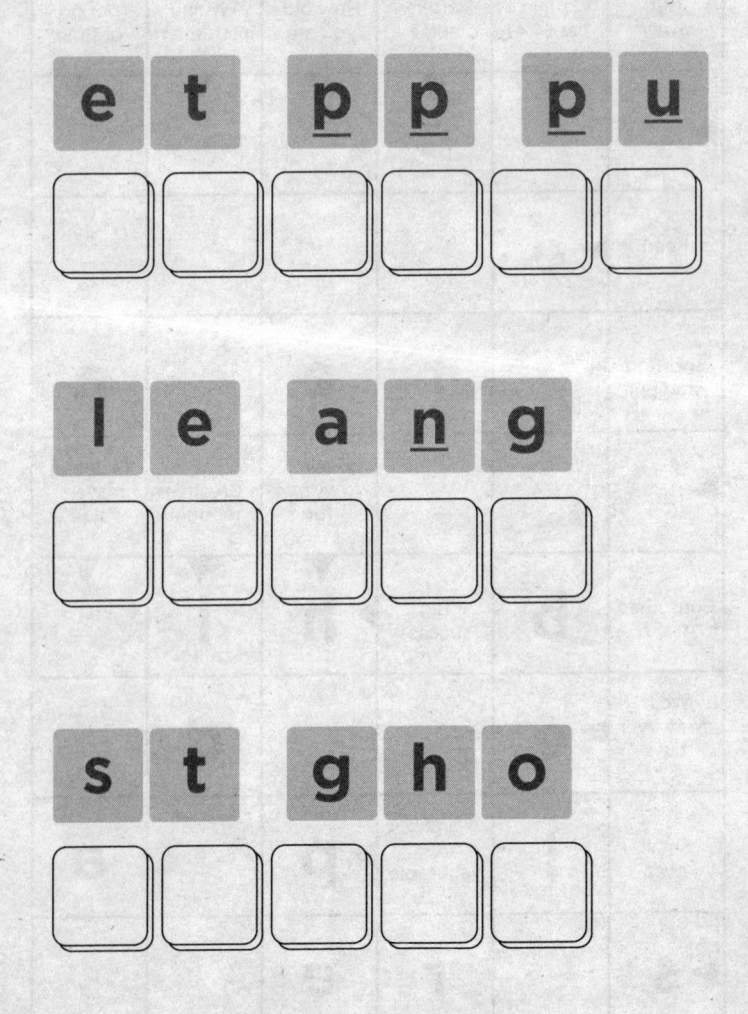

e **t** **p** **p** **p** **u**

l **e** **a** **n** **g**

s **t** **g** **h** **o**

ARROW WORDS

Work out the answers to the clues and write them in the grid, following the arrows.

Get away	Safety item worn in a car (4,4)	Look after; nurse	How old you are	Writing instrument	A long period of time
▶	▼	▼ **c**	▼	▼	▼
Keen	▶ **e**				
Sporting stadium	▶	**r**	**e**		**a**
⚑			Desire; wish for	Creative thought	Group of players; side
Consumed food	**b**	Big success	▶ **h**	**i**	▼
Wear away over time	▶ **e**			**d**	
Small river	**l**	Small green vegetable	▶ **p**		**a**
▶ **s**			**r**	**e**	

SNAKEWORD

Draw a continous line through the tiles below to spell out the hidden six-letter word. Any of the tiles could be the first letter, and the line can only pass through each tile once.

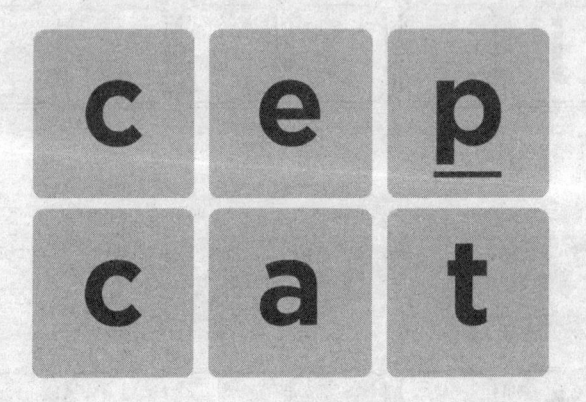

Write the word here.

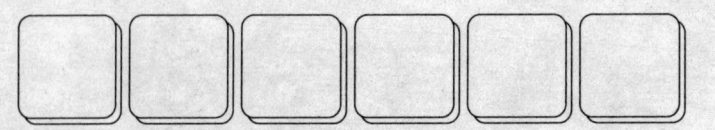

STAR LETTERS

Work out the six-letter word, using each Scrabble tile once and the star tile twice. There are three words for you to find. The first letter has been filled in for you.

WORD DETECTIVE

Link the tiles to make as many words with three letters or more as you can. The letters can be linked in any direction - across, up, down or diagonally but you can't use the same tile twice in one word. Can you find the six-letter word?

y	a	o	<u>n</u>
r	i	e	v
l	g	i	f
<u>q</u>	m	h	<u>p</u>

....
....
....
....
....
....

KRISS KROSS

Place all of the words in the list below into the empty tiles. Use each word once to complete the puzzle.

3 LETTERS
cow
pig

4 LETTERS
calf
eggs

5 LETTERS
crops
field
grain
horse
lambs
sheep

6 LETTERS
farmer
stable

7 LETTERS
tractor

WORDSEARCH

Find all the words from the list below in the grid. Words may appear horizontally or vertically.

t	o	m	a	t	o	p	k
t	e	a	s	o	m	c	l
j	r	s	a	p	e	c	i
z	p	e	p	p	e	r	s
b	a	s	e	i	t	u	o
o	n	i	o	n	r	s	v
t	r	v	y	g	t	t	e
c	h	e	e	s	e	a	n

base
cheese
crust
onion

oven
peppers
tomato
toppings

GIVE ME A CLUE

Can you fill in the blank Scrabble
tiles to complete the words?
Use the clues to help.

Clue 1 Laugh

g ☐ g ☐ ☐ ☐

Clue 2 Type of metal

c ☐ ☐ p ☐ r

Clue 3 Main meal

☐ i ☐ n ☐ ☐

Clue 4 Painter

a ☐ t ☐ ☐ ☐

WORD SCRAMBLE

Rearrange the Scrabble tiles to create four words.
(Hint: They are all words about transport.)

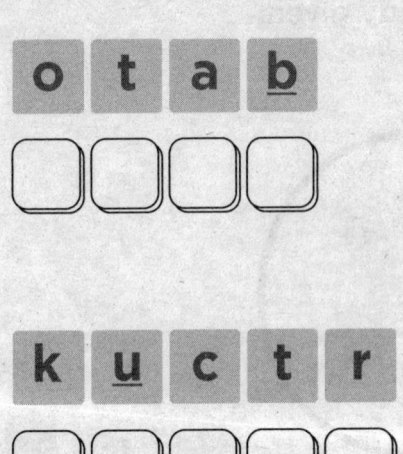

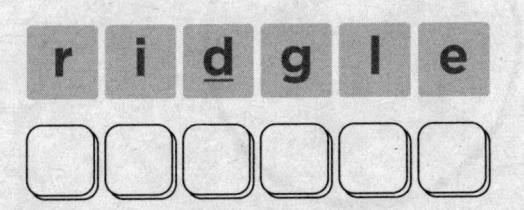

WORD LINK

Use all the letters in the circle to make a word that links onto the word already given.

b i k e

Use all the letters in the circle to make a word that hooks the word already given – making two new words at once!

g a t e

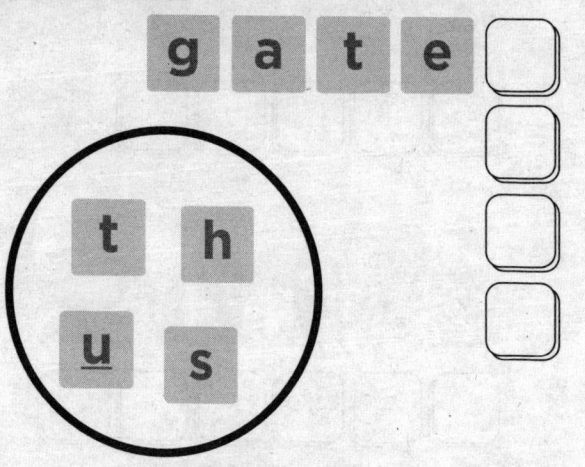

WORD MATCH

Can you unscramble each of the words and then draw a line to match each word with the correct picture?

o t a r r <u>p</u>

c h r o a <u>n</u>

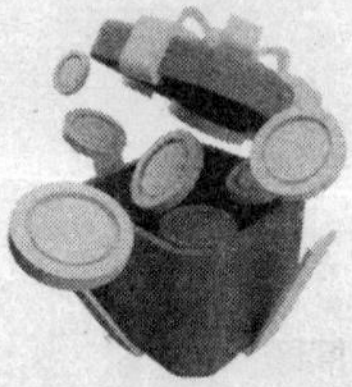

<u>p</u> l k a <u>n</u>

o i c s <u>n</u>

STAR LETTERS

Work out the six-letter word, using each Scrabble tile once and the star tile twice. There are three words for you to find. The first letter has been filled in for you.

v o g e r

g _ _ _ _

i t b r a

r _ _ _ _ _

i e r w n

w _ _ _ _ _

MISSING VOWELS

All vowels have been removed from each word below and are shown at the side. Can you put them back in to recreate the words?

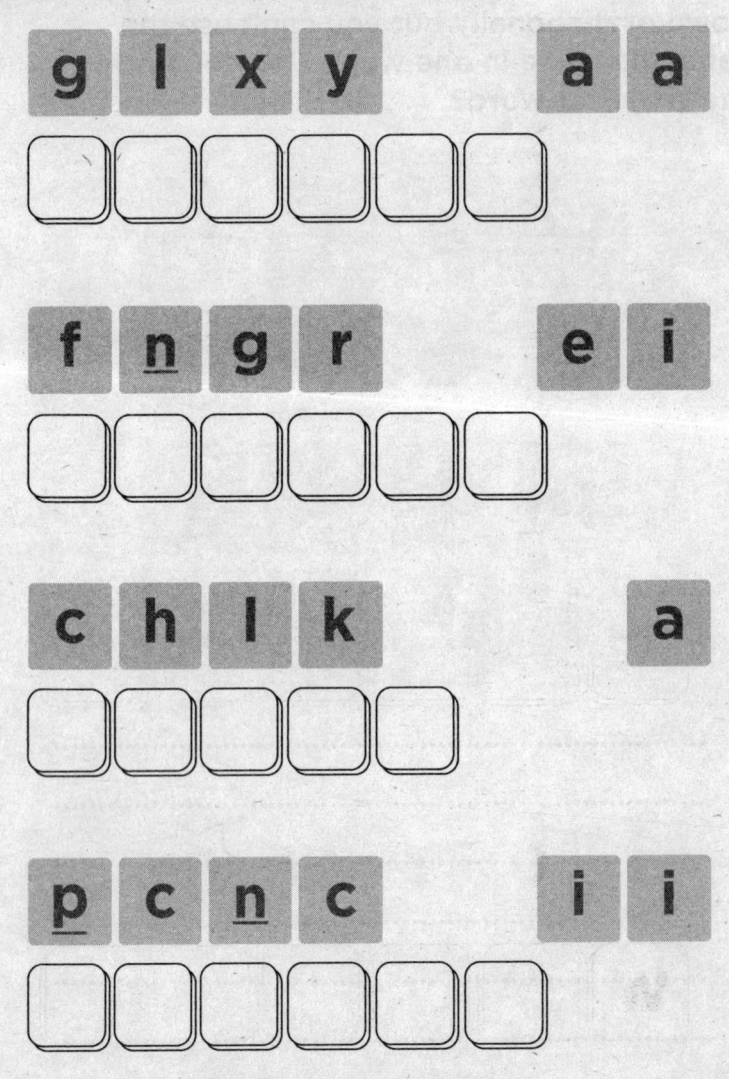

g l x y   a a

☐ ☐ ☐ ☐ ☐ ☐

f n g r   e i

☐ ☐ ☐ ☐ ☐ ☐

c h l k   a

☐ ☐ ☐ ☐

p c n c   i i

☐ ☐ ☐ ☐ ☐ ☐

WORD DETECTIVE

Link the tiles to make as many words with three letters or more as you can. The letters can be linked in any direction - across, up, down or diagonally but you can't use the same tile twice in one word. Can you find the six-letter word?

w	a	r	e
c	z	u	m
p	l	t	l
i	f	u	q

....

....

....

....

....

....

ARROW WORDS

Work out the answers to the clues and write them in the grid, following the arrows.

Slender	Narrow road	Hero	Rug	Rodents with long tails	▼
▶ s	▼	▼ i	▼ m	Large bird	
Change ▶				▼	t
Musical symbols ▶	n			e	
▶	e		Piece of paper in a book		Try out
Sticky liquid put in hair	Chopping tool	Deep hole in the ground ▶	▼		▼ t
▶	▼		a		
Where a king or queen lives	x	E.g. oxygen or nitrogen ▶	g		
Major happening ▶	e	v			

SNAKEWORD

Draw a continous line through the tiles below to spell out the hidden six-letter word. Any of the tiles could be the first letter, and the line can only pass through each tile once.

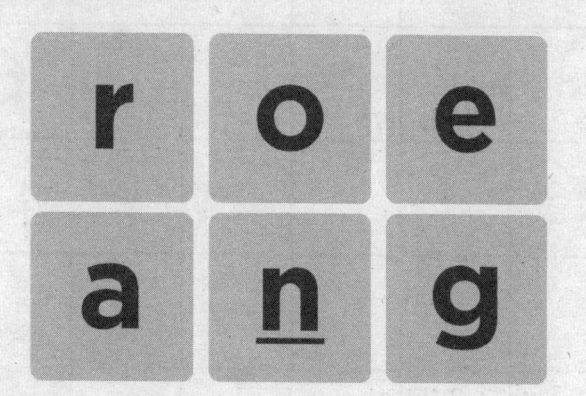

Write the word here.

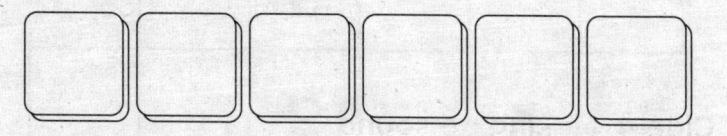

GIVE ME A CLUE

Can you fill in the blank Scrabble
tiles to complete the words?
Use the clues to help.

Clue 1 Season

| a | | | u | | |

Clue 2 Well known

| f | | | o | | |

Clue 3 Get away

| | s | c | | | |

Clue 4 Making no sound

| s | | | | n | |

WORDSEARCH

Find all the words from the list below in the grid. Words may appear horizontally or vertically.

p	a	t	r	j	a	r	a
i	b	r	a	n	c	h	t
n	f	e	r	o	o	t	s
e	m	w	i	l	l	o	w
e	a	m	v	r	y	t	l
a	p	u	o	t	j	w	r
l	l	e	a	f	x	i	o
r	e	s	k	u	e	g	l

branch	pine
leaf	roots
maple	twig
oak	willow

WORD SCRAMBLE

Rearrange the Scrabble tiles to create four words.
(Hint: They are all words about food.)

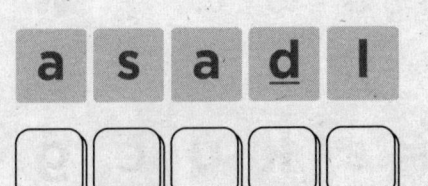

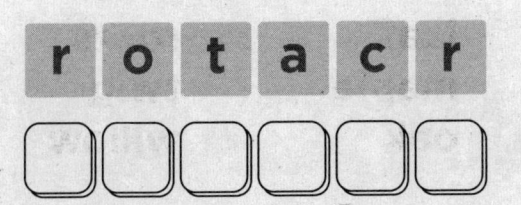

WORD MATCH

Can you unscramble each of the words and then draw a line to match each word with the correct picture?

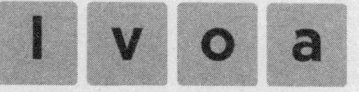

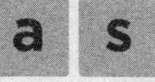  

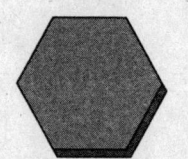

KRISS KROSS

Place all of the words in the list below into the empty tiles. Use each word once to complete the puzzle.

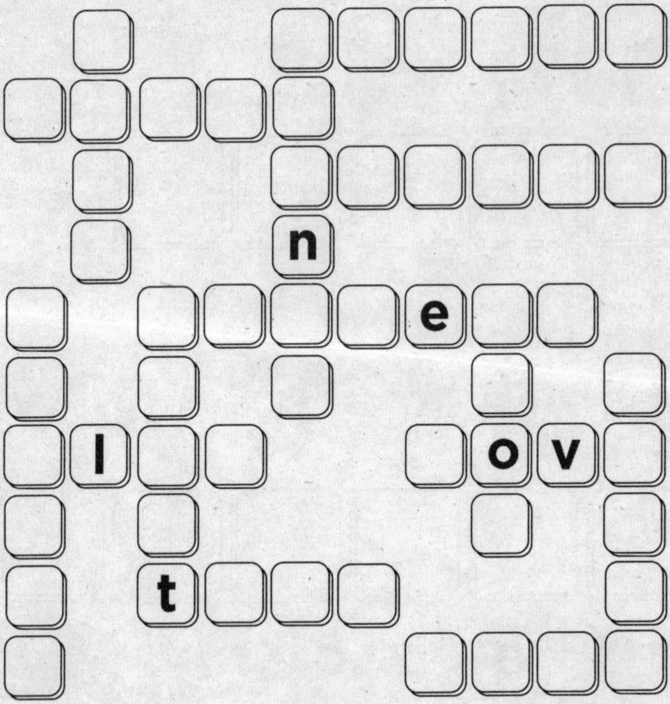

4 LETTERS
have
move
play
show
take
want

5 LETTERS
leave
start
watch

6 LETTERS
appear
change
create
expect

7 LETTERS
suggest

WORD SPLITS

These three words have been split into two or three parts and reordered. Can you put the parts in the right order to make the original word?

r y | s o r

e y | c k | h o

c e | t w i

WORD LINK

Use all the letters in the circle to make a word that links onto the word already given.

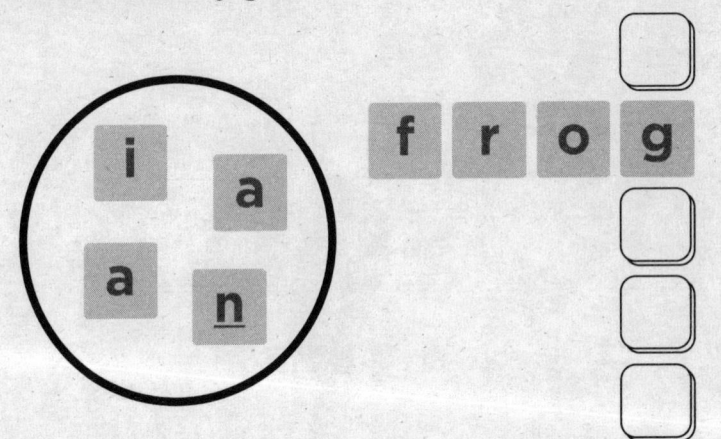

f r o g

Use all the letters in the circle to make a word that hooks the word already given – making two new words at once!

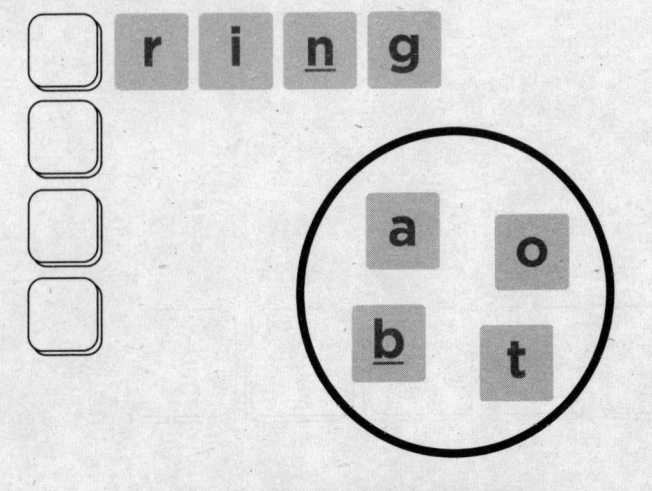

r i n g

BEGINNER PUZZLE ANSWERS

Page 4 – Word Detective

six-letter word

advice

there are lots of other possible words e.g.

jar, legs, seal and alter

Page 6 – Give me a Clue

1 start
2 eagle
3 chess
4 enter

Page 5 – Arrow Words

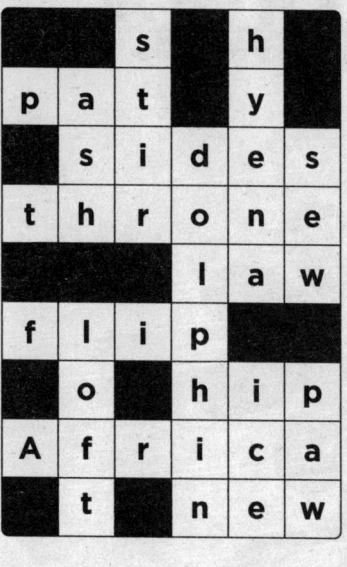

Page 7 – Kriss Kross

Page 8 – Missing Vowels

dizzy
window
shrimp
wizard

Page 10 – Word Match

s l o t h

s h e e p

s p i d e r

s n a k e

Page 9 – Snakeword

donkey

Page 11 – Star Letters

jelly
steep
hobby

Page 12 – Word Scramble

lion
camel
horse
rabbit

Page 14 – Wordsearch

a	a	q	a	t	t	e	k
l	i	v	e	r	e	q	i
t	a	n	k	l	e	n	d
c	s	w	g	y	t	e	n
t	m	o	u	t	h	c	e
s	e	s	h	a	e	k	y
h	a	n	d	l	p	o	s
r	r	t	h	n	s	u	s

Page 13 – Word Splits

banana
tulip
double

Page 15 – Word Link

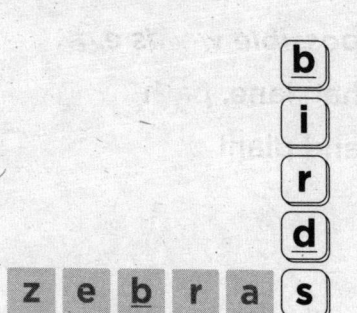

b
o
o
k i t e

b
i
r
d
z e **b** r a **s**

Page 16 – Arrow Words

	w				u
	a	p	r	o	n
	s	e	e		d
	t	e	a	s	e
c	e	l	l	a	r
				f	
	d	e	c	a	y
	a	w	a	r	e
	m	e	r	i	t

Page 18 – Kriss Kross

s a n d w i c h — c
u — h a r t
b e l l — r — i
j — e — r — r
e — s — a — b
c — s t u d y — o
t — o — i — o
— n — n — k
d e s k — g a m e s

Page 17 – Word Detective

six-letter word
happen

there are lots of other
possible words e.g.
hat, lane, path
and plant

Page 19 – Word Match

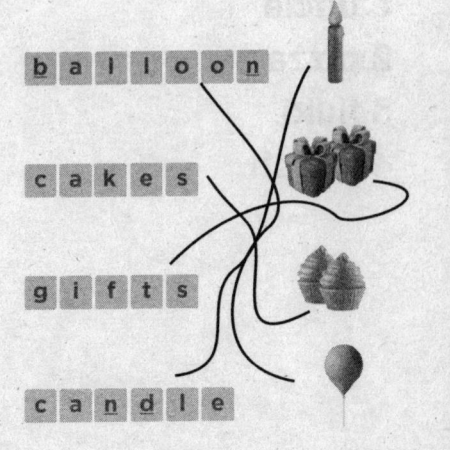

b a l l o o n

c a k e s

g i f t s

c a n d l e

Page 20 – Star Letters

wheel
funny
igloo

Page 22 – Snakeword

change

Page 21 – Give Me a Clue

1 uncle
2 pizza
3 fluid
4 beach

Page 23 – Word Scramble

fish
whale
shark
walrus

Page 24 – Word Splits

apple
garden
daisy

Page 26 – Word Link

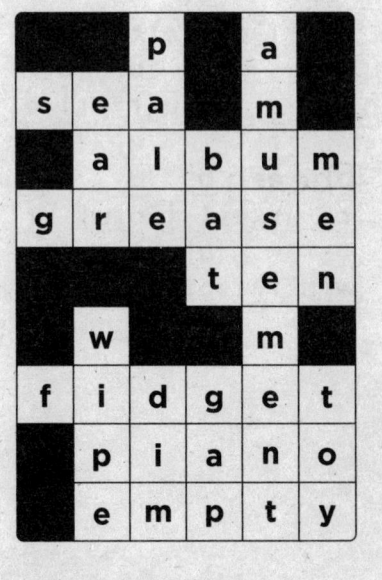

t
r
c a m **p**
i
n
k
e
s t o r m **y**

Page 25 – Wordsearch

b	t	m	e	o	a	u	k
a	w	i	e	m	l	l	j
c	j	l	a	e	l	t	b
o	o	k	h	l	o	a	a
n	c	e	r	e	a	l	n
d	s	l	v	t	s	w	a
e	g	g	s	t	t	a	n
p	j	a	m	e	s	j	a

Page 27 – Arrow Words

		p		a	
s	e	a		m	
	a	l	b	u	m
g	r	e	a	s	e
		t	e	n	
	w		m		
f	i	d	g	e	t
	p	i	a	n	o
	e	m	p	t	y

69 – BEGINNER ANSWERS

Page 28 – Word Detective

**six-letter word
clever**

*there are lots of other
possible words e.g.*
**vet, even, yolk
and kneel**

Page 30 – Word Match

Page 29 – Kriss Kross

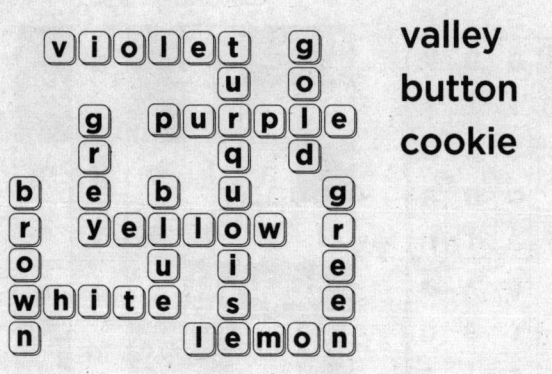

Page 31 – Star Letters

**valley
button
cookie**

Page 32 – Wordsearch

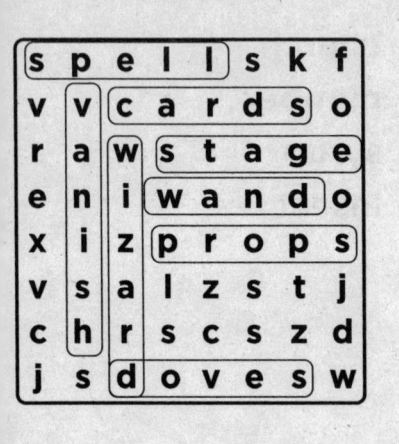

```
s  p  e  l  l  s  k  f
v  v  c  a  r  d  s  o
r  a  w  s  t  a  g  e
e  n  i  w  a  n  d  o
x  i  z  p  r  o  p  s
v  s  a  l  z  s  t  j
c  h  r  s  c  s  z  d
j  s  d  o  v  e  s  w
```

Page 34 – Word Scramble

tree

cards

elves

sleigh

Page 33 – Word Splits

award

coffee

argue

Page 35 – Give Me a Clue

1 lemon

2 above

3 eager

4 puppy

Page 36 – Word Link

g r e e **n**
o
r
t
h

p
a
s e a t
t
a

Page 38 – Missing Vowels

church
number
syrup
insect

Page 37 – Word Match

v i o l i **n**

p i a **n** o

f l **u** t e

g **u** i t a r

Page 39 – Word Splits

puppet
angle
ghost

Page 40 – Arrow Words

e	s	c	a	p	e
	e	a	g	e	r
	a	r	e	n	a
a	t	e			
	b		h	i	t
	e	r	o	d	e
	l		p	e	a
s	t	r	e	a	m

Page 42 – Star Letters

juggle
tennis
spooky

Page 41 – Snakeword

accept

Page 43 – Word Detective

six-letter word
pigeon

*there are lots of other
possible words e.g.*
pie, fear, give
and neigh

Page 44 – Kriss Kross

```
c a l f            s
    a   t          h
f a r m e r        e
i   b   a          e
e g g s   c r o p s
l   r   c   t      t
d   a   c o w   r  a
    p i g   r      b
    n              l
        h o r s e
```

Page 46 – Give Me a Clue

1 giggle
2 copper
3 dinner
4 artist

Page 45 – Wordsearch

```
t o m a t o p k
t e a s o m c l
j r s a p e c i
z p e p p e r s
b a s e i t u o
o n i o n r s v
t r v y g t t e
c h e e s e a n
```

Page 47 – Word Scramble

boat
truck
train
glider

Page 48 – Word Link

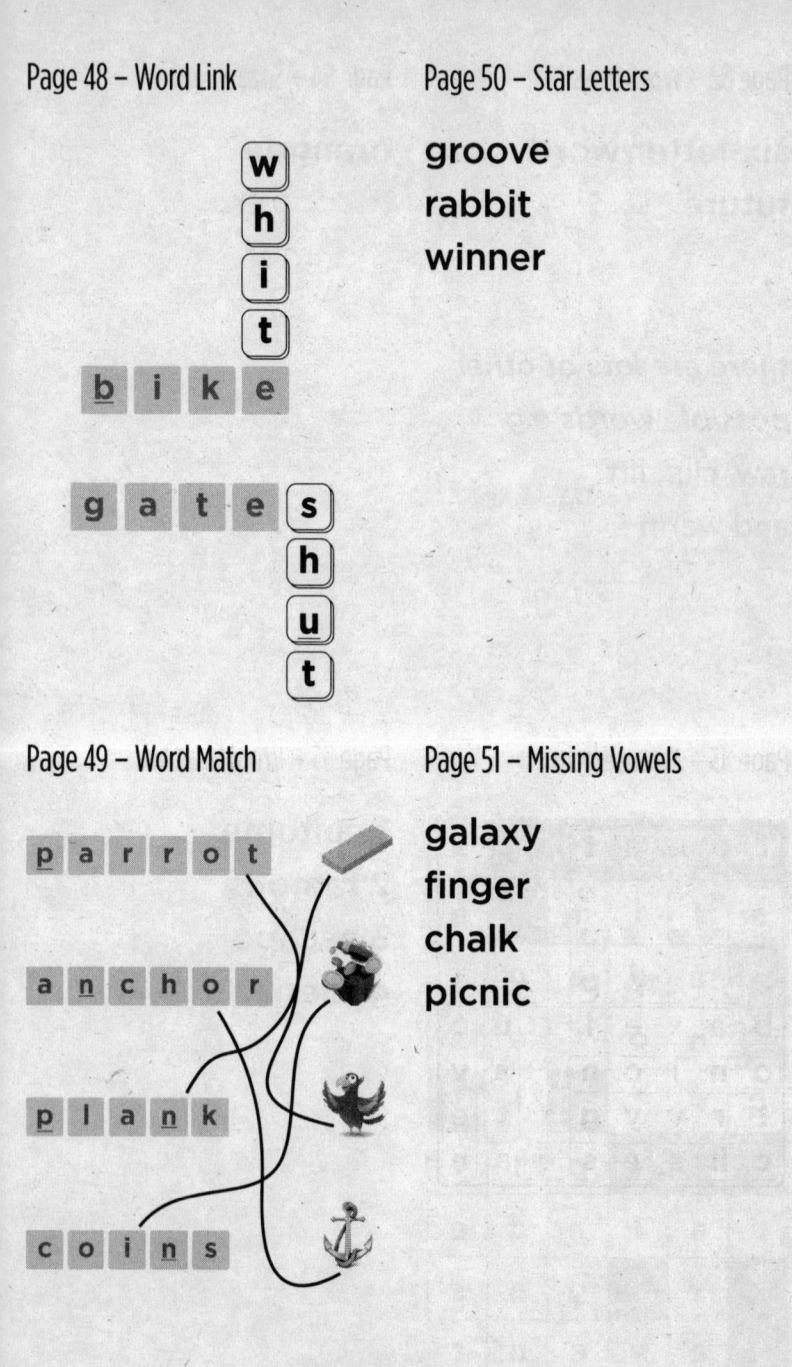

w
h
i
t
b i k e

g a t e s
h
u
t

Page 50 – Star Letters

groove
rabbit
winner

Page 49 – Word Match

p a r r o t

a n c h o r

p l a n k

c o i n s

Page 51 – Missing Vowels

galaxy
finger
chalk
picnic

Page 52 – Word Detective

six-letter word
future

there are lots of other
possible words e.g.
raw, clip, lift
and warm

Page 54 – Snakeword

orange

Page 53 – Arrow Words

					r
s	l	i	m		a
	a	d	a	p	t
	n	o	t	e	s
g	e	l		l	
			p	i	t
p	a	l	a	c	e
	x		g	a	s
	e	v	e	n	t

Page 55 – Give Me a Clue

1 **autumn**
2 **famous**
3 **escape**
4 **silent**

Page 56 – Wordsearch

```
p a t r j a r a
i b r a n c h t
n f e r o o t s
e m w i l l o w
e a m v r y t l
a p u o t j w r
l l e a f x i o
r e s k u e g l
```

Page 58 – Word Match

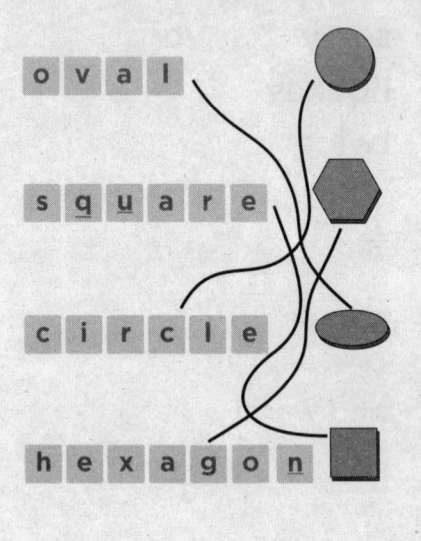

o v a l

s q u a r e

c i r c l e

h e x a g o n

Page 57 – Word Scramble

cake

chips

salad

carrot

Page 59 – Kriss Kross

```
w       c r e a t e
w a t c h
    n       a p p e a r
    t       n
e   s u g g e s t
x   t       e   h   l
p l a y   m o v e
e   r       w   a
c   t a k e     v
t           h a v e
```

Page 60 – Word Splits

sorry

hockey

twice

Page 61 – Word Link

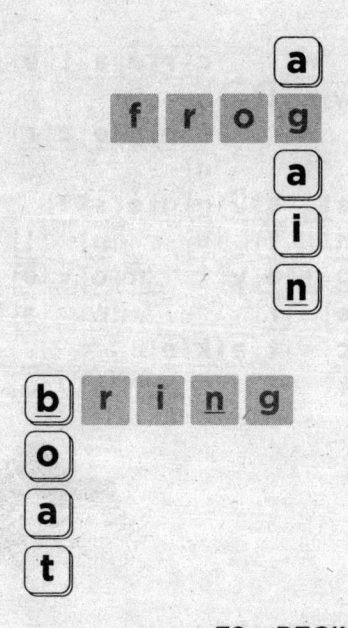

NOTES

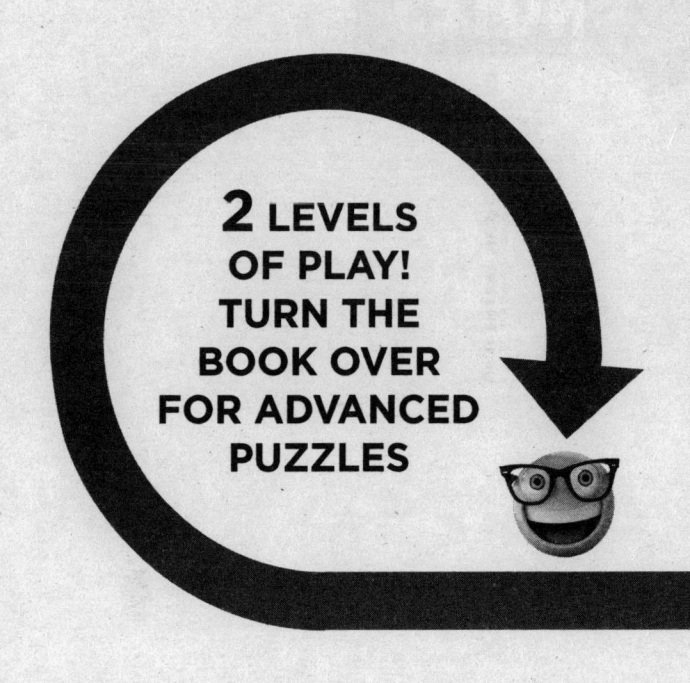

2 LEVELS OF PLAY! TURN THE BOOK OVER FOR ADVANCED PUZZLES

2 LEVELS OF PLAY! TURN THE BOOK OVER FOR BEGINNER PUZZLES